BEcoming:

The Essence of Your True Self

Waking Up with Who You Are

Richard Davies

Dedication

To,

Tom Donaghy, my human services partner in our Youth Leadership work. He sparked my being space…

Keith Ayers (integro.com.au), who projected me further in my work with human behaviour. Thank you so much for your help!

Richard.

Acknowledgment

To all those who have shown me and taught me that what they possess ultimately holds little weight in the end.

To those who courageously understood that it is not what we leave behind in this world, but how we leave it, our essence, our impact that truly matters.

Thank you for your lessons, for trusting me with your vulnerability and your authenticity as a Human being.

This book rests on your Souls.

Contents

Introduction

In a world obsessed with constant productivity, polished images, and public accolades, many of us end up chasing achievements that bring only a flash of satisfaction before fading away. We measure our worth by output instead of presence, by digital approval instead of inner peace, and by how quickly we check items off our endless to-do lists. Yet beneath all the noise and speed is something deeper and timeless, a still, steady voice reminding us, "You are more than what you achieve. You are more than you do."

"BE coming: The Essence of Your True Self" is more than a book... It is a profound guide to rediscovering the intrinsic values that define your existence. It's about finding the deeper reasons that get you out of bed each morning and energize you to step fully into life. The book explores the fundamental question of identity by encouraging readers to delve deep into the heart of their being, moving past superficial desires and societal expectations. With a blend of insightful anecdotes, philosophical musings, and practical exercises, it leads you on a transformative journey to uncover your true purpose, desires, and aspirations, not defined by possessions or professional titles, but by the authenticity of who you are. This enlightening read aims to foster self-awareness, authenticity, and fulfillment, inspiring individuals from all walks of life to embrace their essence and live with clarity and courage.

This book is a call to return, not backward into the past, but inward to the center of your being. It's not about adding more to your life; it's about peeling back the layers to discover what's always been there: your true self. If you've ever felt buried beneath the expectations of others or questioned whether your life truly reflects your soul, this is your invitation to begin again.

With each chapter, I will explore what it means to live from the inside out, where authenticity guides every choice. Through stories, practices, and reflections, you will learn to meet yourself with honesty, curiosity, and compassion. You are not here to become someone else. You are here to become you.

Chapter 1

We are taught from a young age to chase goals: grades, careers, titles, and possessions. From the moment we can walk and talk, the world begins measuring us through test scores, gold stars, trophies, and polite applause. The message is quiet yet relentless: **success equals worth**. We're praised when we produce, when we win, when we exceed expectations. And so, brick by brick, we construct an identity out of achievement. We learn to mistake accomplishment for love, to see validation as proof that we are enough.

"You were not born to impress. You were born to express. Be the real you." — Unknown.

"Achievement is not what makes you whole. Wholeness is what makes achievement meaningful." — Brianna Wiest.

As children, we internalize this script long before we even understand what we're agreeing to. As teenagers, we double down, pushing harder to enter the right schools, secure the right internships, and impress the right people. And as adults, we often find ourselves trapped in a relentless chase for more. More titles. More accolades. More evidence that we matter.

But what happens when we reach these milestones and still feel empty?

What happens when the corner office, the six-figure income, or the social media applause leaves us with a quiet ache we can't explain?

This chapter invites you to pause and ask a question we're rarely encouraged to consider:

What am I really chasing—and why?

The Illusion of Arrival

Many of us live with the idea that happiness is just one achievement away.

"We must be willing to let go of the life we planned so as to have the life that is waiting for us." — Joseph Campbell.

"Happiness is not a goal…it's a by-product of a life well-lived." — Eleanor Roosevelt.

We tell ourselves: **"I'll finally feel whole once I finish this degree. I'll relax when I get the promotion. Once I buy the house, everything will fall into place."** But the finish lines keep moving. Each goalpost reached is replaced by another. This treadmill of achievement can be exhilarating for a time, but eventually, it leaves us depleted, wondering why fulfillment slips through our fingers so quickly.

You'll meet people in life who, on paper, have "made it." Take a lawyer who climbed the ranks only to dread Mondays. A startup founder celebrated on magazine covers but was privately battling anxiety. A mother who checked every box society handed her—and then sat in her kitchen one quiet morning, wondering why she felt invisible in her own life.

Their stories highlight a universal truth: **external success does not guarantee internal fulfillment.**

"There is no success if you're disconnected from yourself." — Oprah Winfrey.

"Many people die with their music still in them." — Oliver Wendell Holmes Sr.

The Culture of Performance

This dissonance between outer success and inner emptiness isn't a personal shortcoming; it's the product of a cultural script we've all been handed. We live in a society that glorifies the hustle, rewards burnout, and confuses busyness with significance. We're encouraged to build resumes, not lives. We're urged to build resumes instead of lives, to collect titles instead of truths.

"Your value doesn't decrease based on someone's inability to see your worth." — Unknown.

"We live in a culture where being busy is a badge of honour. But busy doesn't equal fulfilled." — Courtney Carver.

Add to that the curated world of social media, where everyone else's highlight reel becomes the yardstick we measure our own lives against. No wonder we feel behind. No wonder we feel like we're never doing or being enough.

But here's the shift:

Fulfillment isn't something we find at the top of a mountain. It's something we cultivate from within.

"Careers are a sprint. But your life is a marathon. Pace yourself with purpose." — Unknown.

Intrinsic vs. Extrinsic Motivation

At the heart of this exploration is the difference between **extrinsic motivation,** doing something for reward or recognition, and **intrinsic motivation,** doing something because it feels deeply meaningful or joyful.

"The privilege of a lifetime is to become who you truly are." — Carl Jung

When our actions align with our true selves, fulfillment follows. We move from striving to living. From proving to being. From chasing success to embodying it in a way that nourishes, not depletes.

"What you are will show in what you do." — Thomas Edison

"Don't trade your authenticity for approval." — Unknown

A New Vision of Success

This chapter closes with a visualization to help you re-imagine success not as something outside of yourself, not as a future milestone you need to reach, but as something you can choose to live now.

"Success is liking yourself, liking what you do, and liking how you do it." — Maya Angelou.

Imagine a version of your life where your values, not your achievements, shape your days.

Picture yourself waking up in the morning, grounded in purpose, not pressure.

Feel the difference between performing and belonging. Visualize success as presence, connection, authenticity, and peace.

"Don't be satisfied with stories, how things have gone with others. Unfold your own myth." — Rumi.

You don't have to opt out of ambition to reclaim meaning. But you may need to redefine what winning looks like.

Because real success isn't about climbing higher—it's about coming home to yourself.

"And now that you don't have to be perfect, you can be good." — John Steinbeck.

Exercises in Self-Discovery

To begin reconnecting with what truly matters to you, not what you've been told should matter, consider the following invitations:

1. Create a timeline of your major life achievements.

Next to each one, jot down how you *felt* at the time. Did it bring genuine joy, or just temporary pride? Did it align with your values or someone else's expectations?

"Success is only meaningful and enjoyable if it feels like your own." — Michelle Obama.

2. Reflect on moments of true fulfillment.

These might not have come with applause. They could be as simple as a quiet morning with coffee, helping a friend, or getting lost in a creative flow. What made these moments feel real? What values were alive in you then?

"Enjoy the little things, for one day you may look back and realize they were the big things." — Robert Brault

3. Ask yourself: "If no one were watching, what would I still want to do?"

Strip away the performance. Imagine a life lived for presence, not praise. **What would shift? What would stay?**

"The reward for conformity is that everyone likes you but yourself." — Rita Mae Brown.

Chapter 2

Listening To The Inner Voice

Each of us has an inner compass, a quiet guide often drowned out by the external world.

This chapter invites you to slow down and reclaim the art of listening to your intuition… the steady, persistent whisper of your soul.

Underneath the noise of daily life, there is a quiet voice that speaks our truth. Here, we discuss how to tune in to that inner guidance, recognize the language of intuition, and interpret the messages woven into our emotions and bodies. Through reflective exercises, readers begin to reconnect with their innate wisdom.

We explore how intuition communicates through bodily sensations, dreams, emotions, and gut feelings. You'll learn to distinguish between the voice of fear and the voice of wisdom. Practices such as silent walks, intuitive journaling, and mindful meditation help you sharpen your inner listening and trust the wisdom already within you.

You'll also explore the science behind intuitive insight, how the subconscious processes information before our rational mind catches up, and how learning to trust this wisdom can change the trajectory of your choices.

This chapter is about building trust in yourself. When you begin to honor and follow your inner voice, you step onto a path of deep alignment, even if it doesn't always make sense to those around you. You'll learn that clarity often comes not from logic, but from listening. There is a stillness within each of us—a steady flame that never extinguishes, even amid the chaos of modern life. This flame is your inner voice, your intuitive self, the quiet whisper of your soul. It speaks not in shouts, but in nudges, not in words, but in feelings. Often, we miss it. Not because it's absent, but because the world is loud and we've forgotten how to listen.

Here's an invitation to slow down. To turn inward. To soften the noise of expectation, obligation, and distraction—and tune in to the sacred intelligence that resides within you.

"The quieter you become, the more you can hear." — Ram Dass

Reclaiming the Lost Art of Inner Listening

Your intuition is not something you acquire; it's something you remember. It's the innate compass you were born with, long before anyone told you how to think, behave, or decide. But as we grow, we often trade inner knowing for external validation. We learn to ask, "What should I do?" instead of, "What feels right to me?"

But beneath the mental chatter and emotional static, your inner voice is always speaking. The real question is: Are you listening?

Intuition often arrives quietly—through a gut feeling, a shiver down your spine, a moment of clarity in a dream, or a deep sense of knowing that defies explanation. It may not always feel convenient, but it is always honest. And learning to hear it again is not about effort—it's about presence.

"At times, you must leave the noisy confusion of the world and become still. Only in stillness can you hear the voice within." — Regina Brett

How Intuition Speaks: The Language of the Soul

Your inner voice communicates through:

- **Bodily Sensations**: A tight chest may signal misalignment; a sense of lightness may indicate truth. The body knows before the mind understands.

- **Dreams and Symbols**: The subconscious reveals messages through imagery, often metaphorical, inviting exploration rather than immediate analysis.

- **Emotions**: Emotions are messengers. When honoured rather than suppressed, they become portals to deeper truth.

- **Gut Feelings**: Sometimes you just know, not because of logic, but because of resonance.

"There is a voice that doesn't use words. Listen." — Rumi

To sharpen your sensitivity to these signals, begin to build intentional practices:

- **Silent Walks**: Walk without music or distraction. Let nature speak. Let your thoughts flow like a river, unjudged and uninterrupted.

- **Intuitive Journaling**: Let your hand move freely. Don't censor. Ask a question and write whatever comes. Often, the pen reveals what the mind resists.

- **Mindful Meditation**: Sit. Breathe. Witness. In the spaciousness of your breath, your deeper voice will emerge.

"Mind is everything. What we think, we become." - <u>Buddha.</u>

The Science Behind Intuition

Modern neuroscience supports what ancient wisdom has long known: our subconscious often processes information faster than our conscious mind. The brain forms intuitive insights by rapidly analyzing patterns, recalling experiences, and reading emotional cues— often before we're even aware of it.

According to psychologist Gerd Gigerenzer, intuition is not irrational; it's intelligence in a different form, "fast and frugal," as he calls it. Learning to trust this can shift your decision-making from merely reactive to deeply resonant.

Building a Relationship of Trust

At the heart of intuitive living is **self-trust**. It's the courage to honor what you feel, even when it contradicts what others expect. It's choosing alignment over approval. And in a world that thrives on conformity, such authenticity is nothing short of radical.

This doesn't mean every inner whisper leads to ease—sometimes, it will lead you straight into the fire. Yet it is always a fire that forges, not one that destroys. You begin to realize: your inner voice isn't trying to keep you comfortable. It's trying to keep you whole.

"Don't let the noise of others' opinions drown out your own inner voice." — Steve Jobs.

The Wisdom of Listening

Clarity doesn't always come from logic. Often, it comes from surrender—from pausing long enough to hear what's been there all along. When you begin to listen deeply, the path becomes clearer. Not because all doubt disappears, but because your trust in yourself grows stronger than your need for certainty.

This chapter is about remembering what you already know. Rebuilding the bridge between your mind and your soul and stepping forward, not with fear, but with a quiet, rooted confidence.

You are your own compass. Always.

Reflective Exercises: Strengthening Inner Listening

1. The Intuition Check-In

Daily Practice (5–10 minutes)

Each morning or evening, find a quiet moment. Place your hand on your heart or belly. Take three deep breaths.

Ask yourself:

- **What do I need to hear right now?**
- **What am I feeling beneath the surface?**
- **Where in my body do I feel tension, ease, or resistance?**

Don't try to solve or analyse, just listen. Write down whatever comes, even if it feels small or unclear. Over time, patterns will emerge.

2. Inner Voice vs. Inner Critic

Journaling Prompt

Think of a recent decision or moment of self-doubt.

Reflect:

- **What did my inner voice say?**
- **What did my inner critic say?**
- **How did each feel in my body?**
- **Which voice felt more grounded, and why?**

Understanding the emotional and physical tone of each "voice" helps you distinguish wisdom from fear.

3. Dream Mapping

Weekly Practice

Keep a notebook or voice recorder near your bed. When you wake up, record any dreams, symbols, or feelings, even fragments.

At the end of the week, reflect:

- **What symbols keep appearing?**
- **How might these images be metaphors for my inner state?**
- **What might my subconscious be trying to tell me?**

Intuition often whispers through dreams before the waking mind is ready to understand.

4. Follow the Whisper

Intuitive Action Step

Think of something your intuition has been quietly nudging you toward—maybe a creative idea, a hard conversation, or a need for rest.

Ask yourself:

- **If I trusted this nudge fully, what would I do next?**
- **Then do one small action toward it. It doesn't have to be bold, just honest.**

Taking aligned action builds a deeper relationship with your inner voice. Each time you follow it, you strengthen your inner trust.

5. Intuitive Letter Writing

Journaling Practice

Write a letter to yourself from the voice of your intuition. Use the phrase:

"Dear one, this is what I want you to know…"

Let your pen move without overthinking. This voice is kind, compassionate, and wise. Let it speak.

"Go within. There lies the fountain of good." — Marcus Aurelius.

Chapter 3

Unpacking The Mask: Shedding The Roles That Hide Your True Self

From childhood, we learn to adapt. We all wear masks, roles, and personas we adopt to be accepted, to belong, to survive. But over time, these masks can harden into prisons, keeping us from expressing who we truly are.

We wear masks to survive, to belong, to be loved. Over time, these masks harden into identities we mistake for truth. This chapter invites you to look at the roles you've been playing: The Good Child, The Overachiever, The Caretaker, and ask: Who am I without this?

From the moment we arrive in the world, we begin learning how to fit in. We study faces, tones, reactions, absorbing the rules of acceptance like silent apprentices. Slowly, we shape shift. We become what others need us to be: the agreeable child, the peacemaker, the achiever, the strong one. These adaptations become the carefully crafted personas that keep us safe, loved, and included.

Yet safety has a cost. Masks, once protective, can eventually obscure the face beneath.

But masks, though protective, eventually suffocate.

We forget that they were once choices. We start to believe they are us.

"We all wear masks, and the time comes when we cannot remove them without removing some of our own skin."— André Berthiaume.

This chapter invites you into the courageous, tender process of removing those masks not all at once, but gently, layer by layer. Here, we begin asking the quiet, powerful question: **Who am I underneath all this performance?**

Through guided reflection and storytelling, you'll begin to identify the ways you've contorted yourself to meet others' expectations. We also explore the liberation that comes from authenticity and how vulnerability, though uncomfortable, becomes the doorway to deeper connection and inner peace. Practical exercises will help you gently peel back these layers to uncover the essence beneath.

This chapter invites you to examine the roles you've played. Were you the good child, the high achiever, the caregiver? What parts of yourself did you silence to maintain those roles?

Through reflection and storytelling, you'll begin to peel back the layers of performance. You'll also learn how these identities, though once necessary, may no longer serve who you are becoming. We explore how societal and familial expectations shaped the versions of ourselves we thought we had to be.

The Roles We Inherit and Adopt

Adapting to our environment is a natural human instinct. But when adaptation becomes identity, we risk losing touch with our essence.

You may recognize yourself in one or more of these common roles:

- **The Good Child**: You learned that love came when you were obedient, polite, and undemanding. So, you silenced your needs to avoid rocking the boat.
- **The Overachiever**: You equated worth with productivity, chasing perfection to feel valid.
- **The Caregiver**: You found purpose in serving others, but somewhere along the way, your own needs were buried.
- **The Chameleon**: You mastered blending in, reading every room with expert precision, but at the cost of your own truth.

These roles were not born from weakness. They were born from wisdom, crafted to keep you safe in environments where your full self may not have been welcomed.

"We are not born with a mask, but we learn to wear one when we believe our true face will not be loved." — Unknown.

What Did You Hide to Belong?

To sustain the mask, something had to be sacrificed: a dream left unspoken, an opinion swallowed, a wildness restrained, a vulnerability suppressed.

Reflect on what you had to silence to be accepted. Perhaps it was your sensitivity, your anger, your identity, or even your need to rest. These buried parts are not weaknesses; they are doorways back into your wholeness.

When the Mask No Longer Fits

There comes a point when the mask begins to chafe. You feel the weight of inauthenticity pressing against your chest. You say "yes" when you mean "no," smile when you feel hollow, and achieve while secretly longing for something more.

This discomfort is not failure. It's a signal: the soul is stirring. The real you is ready to step forward.

"The privilege of a lifetime is to become who you truly are." — Carl Jung

Shedding the mask is not about rejection of the past, but about integration. It's about honouring who you had to be—and choosing who you now want to become.

Vulnerability: The Path to Liberation

Taking off the mask feels terrifying at first. Vulnerability leaves us exposed. But it also opens the doorway to freedom. To connect. To truth.

When you speak your truth, even if your voice trembles, you create space for others to do the same. When you let yourself be seen as messy, imperfect, and real, you begin to heal.

"Owning our story and loving ourselves through that process is the bravest thing we'll ever do." — Brené Brown.

Vulnerability becomes a pathway to freedom. You'll learn that the more you reveal, the more you heal.

Embracing Imperfection

Perfectionism tells us we must be flawless to be worthy. Yet your imperfections are not flaws at all; they are the fingerprints of your humanity.

Perfectionism is a mask of fear. In our attempt to be flawless, we disconnect from what makes us real. This chapter invites you to unlearn the toxic belief that worthiness depends on perfection and to discover how mistakes, flaws, and even messiness are not problems to solve, but portals to growth and connection.

We examine the roots of perfectionism, often stemming from shame and fear of judgment. Through real-life stories, you'll see how embracing imperfection can transform lives, and through practical exercises, you'll learn to practice and encourage self-compassion, forgiveness, and the celebration of progress over perfection. Here, we learn to hold ourselves tenderly and embrace our full humanity.

This chapter helps you confront the roots of perfectionism: shame, fear, and the desire to control. You'll meet real people who found liberation not in fixing themselves, but in embracing their messiness.

We explore how mistakes and vulnerability foster growth, resilience, and creativity. You'll learn to reframe "failure" as feedback and recognize strength in softness.

You'll be invited into practices of self-compassion, forgiveness, and truth-telling. Here, we uncover how your greatest gifts often lie hidden within what you once believed were weaknesses. And when you stop striving to be perfect, you finally create the space to become whole.

Closing Invitation: From Armor to Freedom

The mask served its purpose. It got you through. But it's no longer who you are.

You are allowed to let it go.

You are allowed to be seen in all your realness, messiness, softness, and power.

Because the more you reveal…The more you heal.

You are not your performance. You are not the roles you learned to play. You are something deeper, wilder, more beautiful, and truer.

Removing the mask takes courage. But behind it, your real face is waiting with all its brilliance, its softness, its fierce clarity.

It's time to meet yourself again.

Guided Exercises: Gently Peeling Back the Layers

1. Letter from a Role

Choose one of your past roles, perhaps The Perfectionist, The Peacemaker, or The Strong One. Write a letter from this role to your current self.

Prompt:

"Dear [Your Name], I was created to protect you. Here's what I did for you, what I feared, and what I'm ready to let go of..."

Journal Space:

____

____

____

____

____

____

____

2. The Risk of Being Real

Think of a moment when you chose truth over fitting in. When you let yourself be seen.

- What happened?
- How did it feel?
- What did you gain, even if it was uncomfortable?

Journal Space:

---

3. Mirror Truth Meditation

Stand before a mirror. Look gently into your own eyes. Speak aloud:

"This is me. Without the mask. And I am enough."

Repeat it slowly. Feel the truth of the words in your body. Let any emotion rise without judgment.

Reflection Prompt:

How did this feel? What did you notice?

Journal Space:

____

____

____

____

____

____

____

4. Identity Inventory

Roles I've Played	What They Cost Me
e.g. The Overachiever	Rest, Playfulness
e.g. The Caregiver	Emotional Boundaries
e.g. The Chameleon	A Clear Sense of Self

5. Wild Self Visualization

Close your eyes. Imagine the version of you who never needed to perform. Who feels free? Who speaks from the soul. What do they look like? How do they move? What do they know?

Now write from their voice:

"I am your unmasked self, and I want to remind you…"

Journal Space:

Reflection: What's Beneath the Mask?

Take a moment to answer these questions in your journal or the space below.

1. **What roles did you learn to play in childhood?** What did they protect you from? What did they cost you?

Journal Space:

---

2. What parts of yourself did you suppress to maintain these roles?

Think: feelings, needs, dreams, identities.

**"We all wear masks, and the time comes when we cannot remove them without removing some of our own skin."
— André Berthiaume**

Chapter 4

Reclaiming The Now As A Sacred Act

"The present moment is filled with joy and happiness. If you are attentive, you will see it." — Thich Nhat Hanh.

In a world addicted to speed, presence is a radical act. This chapter invites you to pause to stop doing and start being.

We explore mindfulness not as a trendy practice, but as a sacred return to the present moment. You'll practice how to engage your senses, slow your breath, and attune to the quiet rhythms of your life. Practices include mindful eating, digital detoxing, and creating moments of stillness in daily life.

We also address the discomfort that arises when we slow down the anxiety, the urge to distract. You'll learn to meet these edges with compassion, discovering how presence itself becomes a tool for emotional regulation and a wellspring of resilience in the face of stress.

Presence becomes not just a practice, but a way of being, a gateway to peace, clarity, and joy. It opens the door to deeper self-awareness and genuine connection with others.

We often live in a state of autopilot, moving from one task to the next, missing the richness of the present moment. Presence is the key to waking up. It calls us to stop, to breathe, and to simply be.

This chapter is a deep dive into mindfulness practices that help bring awareness to the now.

We explore the science and spirituality of presence, how it calms the nervous system and brings clarity. You'll learn simple practices such as mindful eating, conscious breathing, and digital detoxing. We also address the resistance to slowing down and how to overcome the discomfort that comes with stillness. By cultivating presence, you reconnect with your body, your intuition, and the wonder of simply existing. In a world obsessed with productivity and acceleration, choosing presence is a radical act of rebellion. When the world tells you to keep moving, achieving, producing, presence whispers, pause, it invites you to drop beneath the noise and return to the only place life is truly lived: the now.

This chapter is not about mastering mindfulness as a performance. It's about remembering how to be here, fully, gently, with awareness. It's about returning to the body, the breath, the earth beneath your feet, and the sacredness of simple moments.

Living on Autopilot: The Cost of Disconnection and Managing with Habits

Many of us move through our days without truly arriving in them. We multitask our way through meals, conversations, and even rest. Our bodies are here, but our minds are already somewhere else, planning, replaying, anticipating, escaping.

This disconnection builds as 'habits', and soon, we wonder why we feel numb, exhausted, or hollow inside.

Habits are deeply ingrained patterns of behaviour that are formed through repeated actions. These behaviours are not merely mental routines but have physiological roots in the brain, especially in structures like the basal ganglia, which play a key role in habit formation and motor control. When a person repeatedly performs an action, the brain forms neural connections that make this behaviour easier to repeat with less conscious effort. This process is known as neuroplasticity, the brain's remarkable ability to reorganize itself by creating new neural pathways in response to experience.

As habits are repeated, the pathways associated with these actions become stronger and more efficient. Myelin, a fatty substance that coats nerve fibres, plays a crucial role in this process. When neural pathways are frequently activated, the brain wraps these pathways in myelin, which acts like insulation, allowing electrical signals to travel faster and more efficiently. This makes it easier for the brain to initiate and carry out the habitual behaviour without needing much thought or decision-making. Over time, these myelinated pathways become the default route, making the behaviour almost automatic.

However, this process, while efficient, also carries risks. When habits are formed unconsciously or mindlessly, they can become detrimental. Blind adherence to routine, especially when it reinforces unhealthy or unproductive actions, can harm both physical and mental health. These behaviours often operate below the level of conscious awareness, making it difficult for individuals to change or question them. In extreme cases, habitual actions may override rational thought, leading to behaviour that does not align with one's values or long-term goals. This is particularly true for habits like overeating, substance abuse, or procrastination, where the brain has reinforced patterns of behaviour that are ultimately harmful. Therefore, while habits serve to streamline behaviour and reduce cognitive load, they must be consciously examined and adjusted to avoid the pitfalls of unconscious repetition.

Consider this: 'Have you ever driven, maybe driving to a favourite location for a well-earned Holiday? Arriving at your destination, you found it hard to remember, couldn't even recall the last hour of your driving journey?' … that's autopilot, that's mindlessness, that's habit. So we drive our lives like that. Seems dangerous, doesn't it?

Presence: A Sacred Return to Now

Presence is the antidote. It is the path home.

Presence is not passive. It is a deeply engaged, intentional way of inhabiting life. It means tuning into the hum of your own breath, the taste of your food, the warmth of sunlight on your skin, and the subtleties of your emotions.

Presence is not just a practice, it's a way of being.

"Realize deeply that the present moment is all you ever have. Make the Now the primary focus of your life."

— Eckhart Tolle

The Science of Stillness

"You should sit in meditation for twenty minutes a day. Unless you're too busy, then you should sit for an hour." — Zen Proverb.

Modern neuroscience affirms what mystics and sages have known for centuries: presence soothes the nervous system, lowers cortisol, and brings coherence to the mind and body.

Slowing down is not laziness. It's restoration. When you pause, you signal to your brain that you're safe. This allows your parasympathetic nervous system to activate your "rest and restore" state, supporting healing, emotional regulation, and clarity.

Meeting the Discomfort of Slowing Down

Often, when we attempt to be present, we are met not with peace but with discomfort. Stillness can bring up anxiety, restlessness, or the urge to check out.

This is normal. The mind resists presence because it fears what it might feel when silence descends.

"Almost everything will work again if you unplug it for a few minutes, including you." — Anne Lamott.

Presence asks us to stop running. To feel what we've been avoiding. And to meet it with compassion, not judgment.

"Nothingness haunts Being." — Jean-Paul Sartre.

Presence as a Path to Wholeness

When you begin to live with presence, you start to notice things: the signals of your body, the textures of your emotions, the beauty hidden in ordinary things, the quiet wisdom that rises in silence. You become more connected to yourself, to others, to life itself.

Presence becomes a portal. Not to escape, but to arrive fully awake, fully alive.

"To be present is to be available to life." — Tara Brach

"The ability to be in the present moment is a major component of mental wellness." — Abraham Maslow

Practices for Cultivating Presence

You don't need hours of meditation or a silent retreat. Presence lives in the small, ordinary moments when you choose to be instead of doing.

Mindful Breathing

Sit quietly. Inhale slowly for a count of four. Exhale for a count of six. Repeat for 2–5 minutes. Let your breath anchor you in the now.

Mindful Eating

Eat one meal a day with full attention. No phones, no distractions. Notice taste, texture, and the feeling of gratitude for nourishment.

Digital Detox Moments

Set tech-free zones or times. Begin with 30 minutes before bed. Let silence reclaim your space.

Stillness Pauses

Insert micro-moments of stillness into your day. One deep breath before a meeting. One quiet moment after closing your laptop. Let these pauses become sacred rituals.

Reflective Practices: Welcoming the Now

These journaling prompts and mindfulness exercises will help you deepen your relationship with the present moment.

1. Presence Inventory

Prompt:

> What are three moments today when you felt truly present?
>
> What are three moments you were distracted or on autopilot?

Journal Space:

2. The Pause Practice

Set a timer to go off every 2 hours. When it does, stop. Breathe. Feel your feet. Ask:

- What's happening inside me right now?
- Can I soften, just a little, into this moment?

End-of-day reflection:

What did I notice when I paused?

---

3. Reclaim a Daily Ritual

Choose one daily activity to do with presence—washing your face, making tea, walking the dog.

Prompt:

How does this activity feel when I bring my full awareness to it?

What does it teach me about slowing down?

4. Quote Contemplation

Choose one quote from this chapter. Reflect on its meaning for you. Write a short reflection beginning with:

"What this quote reveals to me is…"

Journal Space:

____

____

____

____

____

____

____

5. Create a Sacred Stillness Space

Designate a corner in your home or day for stillness, a cushion by a window, a chair under a tree, a few moments before sleep.

Let this be your place to return, again and again, to the present.

Final Invitation

Presence isn't something you have to earn. You only must remember.

You are already here.

Life is already unfolding.

This moment is already enough.

Breathe. Come home.

"Drink your tea slowly and reverently, as if it is the axis on which the world earth revolves—slowly, evenly, without rushing toward the future." — Thich Nhat Hanh.

Chapter 5

Values, Passions, And Purpose

What Truly Matters And How to Live It

"Don't ask what the world needs. Ask what makes you come alive, and go do it. Because what the world needs is people who have come alive." — Howard Thurman

What lights you up? What feels meaningful? This chapter guides you through the process of clarifying your values, the non-negotiables that guide your life, and discovering your passions. By understanding what makes you feel alive, you begin to unlock the doorway to purpose.

You'll explore the difference between passion and purpose, and how small sparks of interest can lead to greater clarity. Practical explorations include a values inventory, passion mapping, and visualizing a day lived fully in alignment with your purpose.

This chapter empowers you to live in alignment with what truly matters, rather than chasing what simply looks good on paper. You'll be guided through a values inventory and passion mapping exercise to uncover what lights you up. Together, we'll explore the difference between passion and purpose, and how living in harmony with both creates a life of depth and meaning.

We explore the difference between passion and purpose, and how living in alignment with both creates a life of meaning. What truly matters to you? This chapter is a deep dive into your core values and passions, the compass points that guide your most authentic life.

This chapter also introduces the idea of micro-purpose, how everyday moments of joy, service, and curiosity contribute to a purposeful life.

Purpose doesn't have to be grand or public. Sometimes, it's the quiet devotion to what you love. This chapter reminds you that you don't find purpose—you live it, one choice at a time.

We all long for a life that feels meaningful, a life that reflects who we really are. Yet in a world that rewards appearances, productivity, and prestige, it's easy to lose sight of what matters to *you*.

This chapter is an invitation to pause, turn inward, and ask some of the most important questions you can ask:

What do I truly value? What brings me alive? What am I here to do—not to impress, but to express?

Here, we'll explore how your values, passions, and purpose form the compass that guides your most aligned life.

"Create your future from your future, not your past."

— Werner Erhard.

Values: Your Inner North Star

Your values are the principles you hold most dear, your *non-negotiables*. They are not goals, but guiding truths. When your life is in alignment with your values, you feel grounded, authentic, and fulfilled. When you're out of alignment, you feel stuck, drained, or unmotivated.

"Peace is the result of retraining your mind to process life as it is, rather than as you think it should be." — Wayne Dyer.

Reflection: What Do You Stand For?

Prompt:

List five values you hold most dear. Consider times in your life when you felt proud, fulfilled, or deeply at peace. What values were being honoured?

Examples:

- Integrity
- Freedom
- Growth
- Creativity
- Compassion
- Adventure
- Authenticity

Journal Space:

Now ask yourself:

Which of these am I actively living—and which am I neglecting?

Passion: The Fire That Fuels You

Passion is what excites you. It's what sparks joy, wonder, curiosity, and energy. Passion isn't just about hobbies, it's about what makes you feel alive.

But here's the truth: Passion doesn't always arrive in lightning bolts. Sometimes, it starts as a quiet pull. A flicker. An interest. A sense of *this matters.*

"Passion is energy. Feel the power that comes from focusing on what excites you." — Oprah Winfrey

Passion Mapping Exercise

Step 1: List 10 things that bring you energy or joy. They can be small or large, personal or professional.

Step 2: Circle the ones that make you lose track of time.

Step 3: Ask yourself: What do these passions have in common?

Journal Space:

Your passions point toward your purpose, not because they are the purpose, but because they light the path toward it.

Purpose: Living in Alignment

We often imagine purpose as a grand destiny—an epic mission. But the purpose is more subtle than that. It's not something you find once. It's something you live, choice by choice, day by day.

Purpose is what happens when your values and passions come together in action. It's how you show up for life.

"Purpose is the reason you journey. Passion is the fire that lights your way." — Unknown.

Micro-Purpose: The Everyday Sacred

Not all purposes are loud or public. Some of the most meaningful lives are lived quietly through small acts of kindness, creativity, presence, and service.

- Helping a neighbour.
- Creating beauty through art or words.
- Being fully present with your child.
- Showing up for a friend.

- Tending to your own healing.

These are all acts of purpose. Your life is already filled with them—you just must notice.

"You do not have to wait to be great. You do not need permission to live with purpose. Start where you are—with what you have." — Alex Elle.

Living in Alignment

When your values and passions shape your actions, you begin to live with a sense of inner alignment. Life feels more meaningful—not because it's perfect, but because it's *true*.

You stop chasing what looks good and start choosing what feels right.

You become the kind of person who wakes up not asking,

"What should I do today?"

But instead: **"What would be most meaningful?"**

Reflection Exercises: Clarify and Align

1. Values Inventory

Prompt:

Which five values do I want to live more fully in the next season of my life?

Why are they important to me? What would change if I

honoured them more deeply?

Journal Space:

____

____

____

____

____

____

____

2. Passion Pulse Check

Prompt:

When do I feel most alive? What am I doing? Who am I with? What environments energize me?

What am I doing when I lose track of time?

Journal Space:

____

____

____

____

____

____

____

3. Purpose Visualization

Close your eyes and imagine a day when you live fully aligned with your values and passions.

- What time do you wake up?
- What are you doing?
- How do you feel?
- Who do you connect with?

Describe your purpose-filled day below.

Journal Space:

____

____

____

____

____

4. Aligning the Everyday

Prompt:

What is one small thing I can do today to align with my purpose?

How can I bring more meaning into the ordinary moments?

Journal Space:

5. Your Personal Purpose Statement

Write a one-sentence statement that captures your current sense of purpose.

"My purpose is to… create, nurture, serve, express,

grow, love] by [how you'll do it]."

Example:

My purpose is to nurture connection and healing by creating safe spaces for people to be their true selves.

Your Turn:

Final Reflection

Your values are your compass.

Your passions are your fuel.

Your purpose is the way you walk through the world—with intention, with heart, and with meaning.

You don't have to wait.

You're already on the path.

Keep listening. Keep choosing. Keep becoming.

"At the centre of your being, you have the answer; you know who you are and you know what you want."

— Lao Tzu

Chapter 6

Redefining Success

From Striving to Aligning

Unlearning the World's Version. Embracing Your Own.

"Don't ask what the world needs. Ask what makes you come alive and go do it. Because what the world needs is people who have come alive." — Howard Thurman

Redefining Success

True success isn't measured in metrics—it's measured in alignment. This chapter helps you unhook from society's definition of success and begin to author your own. Whether your path includes climbing the corporate ladder, starting a nonprofit, or living quietly in nature, your success is yours to define.

We explore stories of people who took unconventional paths and found profound fulfillment. You'll be guided through visualizations and exercises that reveal what success means to you, not your parents, not your peers, but the truest part of you. This redefinition brings immense freedom and the courage to follow your unique path.

Success is not a one-size-fits-all destination. This chapter empowers you to redefine it on your own terms.

You'll read stories of people who walked away from conventional paths to pursue something truer. Through visualization and journaling exercises, you'll uncover your unique definition of success—one rooted not in comparison, but in joy, integrity, and resonance.

Success. A word so heavy with expectation, yet so often hollow in experience. We chase it, sacrifice for it, shape our lives around it. But whose definition are we really living by?

In this chapter, we unhook from inherited ideals and craft something far more powerful: a definition of success that is authentic, nourishing, and uniquely yours.

"Success is liking yourself, liking what you do, and liking how you do it." — Maya Angelou.

What does success really mean to you?

For many, success has been handed down like an heirloom wrapped in expectations, polished by culture, and measured in milestones: a degree, a title, a bank balance, a home with matching throw pillows. But what if real success has nothing to do with achievement… and everything to do with *alignment*? What if success isn't about how far you climb, but how deeply you root? Not about what you accumulate, but how much of yourself you *remember* and honour along the way?

This chapter invites you to let go of society's definition of success and craft your own.

What Is Success, Really?

Success is often presented as a destination: a job title, a home, a certain number in your bank account. But many reach that destination only to feel empty. That's because **true success isn't a finish line—it's a feeling. A frequency. A way of being.**

It isn't about how life looks; it's about how life feels when you're living in alignment with your truth.

"Success is peace of mind, which is a direct result of self-satisfaction in knowing you did your best to become the best you are capable of becoming."

— John Wooden

So, what if we let go of society's checklist and built a new blueprint based on joy, meaning, and resonance?

How You Were Taught to Define It

Most of us didn't choose our initial idea of success. It was taught, passed down from family, school, media, and culture. For some, it meant being the provider. For others, it meant prestige. Or perfection. Or productivity.

"We must be willing to let go of the life we planned so as to have the life that is waiting for us." — Joseph Campbell.

But when our worth becomes entangled with performance or approval, we lose sight of our inner compass. We begin to perform life rather than live it.

Unhooking from the Old Blueprint

We're taught to believe success looks a certain way: constant productivity, upward mobility, visible recognition. Yet many of us who've checked those boxes feel restless, disconnected, or quietly dissatisfied.

"It is no measure of health to be well-adjusted to a profoundly sick society." — Jiddu Krishnamurti.

Sometimes we chase success to gain validation. To prove our worth. To quiet the voice that says we're not enough. But external success without internal alignment becomes a hollow victory. It's time to trade striving for sovereignty.

The Difference Between Impressing and Expressing

We often confuse **impression** with **impact**. One is about the image. The other is about essence. A life that impresses others may win applause. But a life that expresses your truth brings peace. And peace is the deepest form of success.

"What if the real measure of success was how whole you feel when no one is watching?" — Anonymous

Let Success Serve You

You are the author of your definition. You get to decide what matters. You get to choose what's enough. And when you do, life begins to expand from the inside out.

"Define success on your own terms, achieve it by your own rules, and build a life you're proud to live." — Anne Sweeney

You don't need to chase the dream handed to you. You can **build the dream that aligns with you**.

"Your life works to the degree you keep your agreements." — Werner Erhard.

The Courage to Disappoint the World

Redefining success is an act of courage. It may mean disappointing people who love you. It may mean letting go of roles you've outgrown. But authenticity always leads to deeper fulfillment.

"You will never truly be free until you no longer need to impress anyone." — Thibaut.

Real success might mean slowing down. Saying no. Starting over. Taking the road less travelled, not because it's easy, but because it's *yours*.

Story Spotlight:

Ana's Redefinition

Ana spent ten years building her dream career as a lawyer. On paper, she had it all. But her body was burning out. Her spirit was dimming. It wasn't until she took a solo sabbatical that she realized: success, for her, was spaciousness. Creativity. Health. Today, she's a wellness coach working part-time, spending her afternoons writing poetry and hiking with her dog. **"I didn't fail,"** she says. **"I just found a better definition."**

Reflection Prompt: Who Defined Success for You?

- Whose voice do you hear when you think about "being successful"?
- What did success mean in your family, culture, or peer group?
- Have you ever achieved something only to find it didn't fulfill you?

Journal Space

Success: A Feeling, not a Finish Line

Real success feels like freedom. It feels like peace, purpose, presence, and passion all woven together. It looks different for everyone, and that's the point.

"Success is not the key to happiness. Happiness is the key to success. If you love what you are doing, you will be successful." — Albert Schweitzer.

We explore the stories of people who stepped off the beaten path:

- A corporate executive who left a high-paying job to teach yoga and found more peace than money ever brought.
- A stay-at-home parent who reclaimed their creativity after decades of people-pleasing.

- A traveller who chose a minimalist lifestyle, finding joy in simplicity over status.

They didn't follow the conventional path. They chose to define their own.

From Impression to Impact

Success often gets confused with impression how things look from the outside. But true fulfillment comes from impact how you live, how you serve, how aligned you are with your soul.

"Don't aim for success if you want it; just do what you love and believe in, and it will come naturally." — David Frost

Ask yourself:

- Am I living to impress… or to express?
- What do I want to *leave behind* in this world, beyond applause or achievement?

Reflection Exercise: Your Success Compass

Step 1: Write down 5 things you were taught to believe define success.

Step 2: Next to each one, write whether this still resonates for *you*.

Step 3: Replace each outdated belief with something truer for your current self.

Example:

- Old Belief: "Success is having a high-paying job."
- True For Me: "Success is having time freedom and work I love."

Journal Space:

The Courage to Live Your Truth

Redefining success often means disappointing others. It may mean stepping into uncertainty, choosing a quieter life, or walking away from the script others expected you to follow. But with that courage comes freedom. When you stop performing, you start living.

"You don't need to prove your worth. You simply need to live it." — Your Inner Voice.

Exercises: Redefine and Reclaim

1. Your Redefinition Statement

Write your own personal definition of success. Make it a mantra, a mission, or a manifesto. Let it reflect your truth. **"Success, to me, means…"**

Keep it where you can see it often: your mirror, journal, or phone lock screen.

2. Visualize a Successful Life On Your Terms

Close your eyes and imagine waking up in a life that feels completely aligned with your values and joy.

- What time do you wake up?
- What does your day include?
- How do you feel throughout the day?
- Who are you with, or are you alone?
- What kind of work, if any, are you doing?

Describe your vision below.

---

3. Micro-Moments of Success

Success doesn't just live in milestones. It lives in moments. List 5 recent moments that felt successful, not because they were big, but because they were real.

Examples:

- Saying no when it was hard.
- Creating something meaningful
- Resting without guilt
- Having a difficult but honest conversation
- Feeling at peace in silence

Your List:

Final Reflection:

What would change in your life if you truly believed you were already enough? What would you pursue if success meant being fully yourself?

Exercises for Redefining Success

1. Your Success Statement

Complete the following sentence and revise it until it feels true. **"To me, success means..."**

(Keep this nearby. Let it become your guiding light.)

2. Micro-Moments of True Success

List 5 recent moments that made you feel deeply fulfilled, not because they were impressive, but because they were *real*.

Example:

- Laughing until you cried with a friend.
- Finishing a creative project
- Being honest in a tough conversation
- Choosing rest instead of pushing
- Feeling at peace in your own skin

Your List:

____

____

____

____

____

____

3. Visualize a Life That Feels Successful

Close your eyes. Imagine your ideal day. One that feels deeply aligned.

Ask yourself:

- What are you doing when you feel most alive?
- What rhythms does your life follow?
- Who are you surrounded by?
- What values are guiding your choices?

Write a short description of your **"success-filled"** life:

____

____

____

____

____

____

____

Closing: Freedom Beyond Approval

You don't need permission to live a life that feels good. You don't need to be the most impressive person in the room. You just need to be the most authentic version of you.

"Success is being yourself fully, without apology." — *Your Inner Knowing*

This chapter isn't about abandoning ambition. It's about aligning your ambition with what truly matters. Success is yours to define. And in doing so, you reclaim your power.

Reflective Journal Prompt:

"What Did I Learn About Success Growing Up?"

- What was praised in your home or culture?
- Whose definition of success did you absorb?
- When did you first feel "not enough"?

Write freely and honestly:

Reflective Exercise: "Success That Looks Good vs. Feels Good"

Good	Feels Good

Success as Resonance

Success isn't one-size-fits-all. It's a deeply personal resonance. When something lights you up, aligns with your values, and brings a sense of quiet satisfaction—that's success.

"Success is when your soul and schedule align." — Brianna Wiest.

What values are guiding your choices?

Write a short description of your "success-filled" life:

64

Chapter 7

Living Your Truth Daily

Knowing who you are is only the beginning. Embodying that truth every day is the practice. This chapter offers tools for living authentically even when it's uncomfortable. From setting boundaries to honouring your rhythms, you'll learn how to integrate your truth into every aspect of life. We tackle common challenges like people-pleasing, fear of rejection, and self-doubt, providing strategies to navigate them with resilience. Daily rituals, affirmation practices, and accountability tools support you in staying aligned. Authentic living becomes a moment-to-moment choice—a practice of courage, presence, and integrity. Awakening to your true self is one thing. Living it, moment by moment, is the real work.

This chapter offers practical tools for daily authenticity: setting boundaries, navigating discomfort, and honouring your natural rhythms. You'll learn how to hold yourself with kindness when fear arises and how to choose truth even when it's hard.

Turning Self-Awareness into Sacred Action

"The privilege of a lifetime is to become who you truly are." — Carl Jung.

Awakening to your true self is a powerful beginning, but it is not the end. Knowing who you are is just the spark. The real transformation comes when you choose to **live** that truth every single day. This chapter is about bringing your inner knowing out into the open through your words, actions, choices, and rhythms. It's about embodying your truth in a world that often asks you to compromise it.

From Knowing to Living

Self-awareness is enlightening. But **self-expression is where the magic lives.** Living your truth means:

- Saying no when you mean no.
- Take breaks when you need them.
- Letting go of roles you've outgrow   n.
- Creating a life that reflects your inner landscape.

"When you show up authentic, you create the space for others to do the same. Walk in your truth." — Unknown.

The Daily Work of Truth

Living authentically is not always comfortable. It's often messy. Vulnerable. Raw. But it is also deeply liberating. You may find yourself navigating fear of rejection, disappointing others, or facing internal resistance. But truth doesn't require perfection—it only asks for presence and practice.

"Tell the truth, or someone will tell it for you." — Stephanie Klein.

Common Roadblocks to Authentic Living

- **People-Pleasing:** Saying "yes" out of guilt instead of alignment.
- **Fear of Judgment:** Silencing your truth to avoid conflict.
- **Self-Doubt:** Questioning if you're "too much" or "not enough."
- **Old Conditioning:** Habits and beliefs that no longer serve who you are becoming.

Accountability Without Shame

This path isn't about being perfectly authentic 24/7. It's about building the muscle of awareness and gently returning to your truth when you drift.

"Fall in love with becoming. The best version of you is always under construction." — Unknown.

Use gentle tools like journaling, trusted friends, or even post-it notes with affirmations to keep you rooted, not as discipline, but as devotion.

Daily Affirmations for Living Your Truth

- I honour what is real for me today.
- I am allowed to grow, shift, and change.
- My truth is valid even if it's uncomfortable.
- I release the need to perform.
- My presence is enough.

Closing: A Way of Walking

Living your truth is not a performance. It's a posture. A sacred way of walking through life, one intentional step at a time.

It's how you move, speak, rest, and love.

It's choosing alignment over approval.

It's answering the question every day:

"What does my truth need from me right now?"

"The soul always knows what to do to heal itself. The challenge is to silence the mind." — Caroline Myss.

"Don't change beliefs. Transform the believer."

— Werner Erhard

Authentic living is not a destination. It is your daily devotion to the truth of who you are.

Reflective Prompt:

"What stops me from living my truth?"

Journal on one or more of the following:

- When do I feel safest to be fully myself?
- Where in life do I hide parts of who I am?
- What would it mean to be honest in all areas of my life?

Honouring Your Rhythms

Living your truth also means honouring your body's needs, your emotional ebbs and flows, and your energetic cycles. It's not about pushing harder, but aligning deeper.

"Rest is not idleness. It is alignment." — Tricia Hersey, The Nap Ministry

Authentic living asks you to listen inwardly before acting outwardly.

Practices for Daily Alignment

Morning Rituals for Grounding

- 3 deep breaths + hand on heart: "What do I need today?"
- Affirmation: "Today, I choose to honour what is real for me."
- Journaling: "If I lived my truth fully today, I would…"

Evening Reflections for Integrity

- What choices felt aligned with my truth today?
- Where did I shrink or self-abandon?
- How can I offer myself compassion and recommit tomorrow?

Boundaries Are Bridges

"Daring to set boundaries is about having the courage to love ourselves, even when we risk disappointing others." — Brené Brown.

Saying no doesn't mean you're selfish. It means you are self-aware. Every "no" to what doesn't serve you is a "yes" to your truth.

Mini Practice: Boundary Clarity

Think of one boundary that would support your truth right now. Say it out loud: "I honour myself by __________."

Example:

"I honour myself by not responding to texts after 9 pm." "I honour myself by saying no to work that drains me."

The Art of Graceful Transitions

As your truth evolves, so will your life. Friendships may shift. Careers may pivot. Relationships may stretch or end. Authentic living requires letting go—not in bitterness, but in grace.

"Your new life will cost you your old one." — Brooke Hampton

Give yourself permission to evolve. Authenticity is fluid. You are not meant to stay the same.

Reflective Exercise:

Where am I out of alignment?

Explore the following areas:

- **Work**
- **Relationships**
- **Health**
- **Spirituality**
- **Creativity**

Ask yourself: What needs to shift? What is no longer true?

Conclusion

The Ongoing Journey

Coming Home to Yourself, Again and Again

"And the day came when the risk to remain tight in a bud was more painful than the risk it took to blossom."

— Anaïs Nin

Becoming your true self is not a finish line to cross. It's not a checklist to complete or a mountain to summit. It is a **lifelong unfolding**, a sacred spiral that circles you inward, turn by turn, deeper, softer, truer. Some days, clarity will flood your bones. On other days, you'll feel lost in the fog. You may take bold leaps forward, then retreat to old patterns. This is not failure; it is the rhythm of awakening. You are a living, breathing becoming.

There will be shedding. There will be a rebirth. You will meet versions of yourself you forgot, feared, or buried. And each time you choose presence over performance, alignment over approval, and truth over fear, you take another courageous step toward wholeness.

"You do not have to be fearless. Doing it afraid is just as brave." — Morgan Harper Nichols.

This book is not a map with one right path. It's a mirror reflecting the wisdom you already carry. The insights, the shifts, the truths you've remembered, those were always within you. You do not need to become someone new. You are simply remembering who you've always been, beneath the noise, beneath the masks.

A Gentle Invitation

Trust your timing. Honor your rhythm. Give yourself permission to begin again—every day. Let your life be a devotion, not a performance. Your choices are rooted in truth, not validation. Let your journey be yours. While **"Man's existence precedes his essence." — Jean-Paul Sartre**, but, in the end, **you are the path**. You are the teacher, the seeker, the sacred unfolding.

"What you are looking for is already in you. You are already everything you are seeking." — Thich Nhat Hanh.

Welcome home. You're not done. You're just beginning again.

Reflective Exercise: Your Three Guiding Words

To BE the Essence You Want to Live By

"Words are seeds. Plant what you want to grow." — Unknown

Purpose:

This exercise helps you distill your intentions for daily living into **three powerful nouns**—essence words that reflect the qualities you want to embody more fully every single day.

Instructions:

1. **Take a few deep breaths** to settle into your body. Let the external world fall away for a moment. Come home to yourself.
2. **Ask yourself:**

o   What truly matters to me right now?

o   How do I want to show up in the world?

o   If someone could feel my energy without me saying a word, what would I want them to feel?

1. Write <u>TWO LISTS</u>
Your <u>FIRST LIST</u> is:

o   **Things I WANT TO 'MAKE SURE I HAVE' in my life**

Exhaust your dreams with everything you'd LIKE TO HAVE. A 5-bedroom mansion, my own children to fill it, a perfect relationship, my Ferrari, beautiful jewelry, two cute sausage dogs, and a Master's Degree… go on until your dreams are complete, and then put your list aside.

2. Then exhaust your <u>SECOND LIST</u> with:

o   **Things I WANT TO 'MAKE SURE I DO' in my life**

Here, you should expand your list to things you WANT TO DO. Dream on and write it down …… I want to complete an international holiday every year, make regular donations to my favourite charity, go to a Live Performance or Theatre every month, get invites to parties, go to the Best Spas, and treat myself to regular 'catch-ups' with Old School Pals to compare our lives, top the leaders board at my Tennis Club ….. go on until your dreams are complete and then put your list aside.

3. Now for your <u>THIRD & FINAL</u> LIST

Another sheet of paper and write a list of THINGS I WANT to BE in MY LIFE

This will be a more challenging list, but it will be the most rewarding once you complete it and believe it.

Write down three nouns—one word each—that represent the energy, values, or emotional truths you want to live by. These could be words like:

- o Peaceful
- o Truthful
- o Joyful
- o Courageous
- o Kind
- o Wise
- o Free

4. **Test your words:**

To know if a word truly resonates with your core values, try this check:

Ask yourself: "Would I ever want to live by the *opposite* of this word?"

If the answer is *no*, you're likely on the right track.

For example:

- o If you choose **truthful**, would you ever want to live by **deception**?

- o If you choose **free**, would **restriction** feel like a life you want to lead? If the opposite feels like something you'd avoid at all costs, then your word likely speaks to something essential within you.

5. **For each noun, reflect briefly on why you chose it:**

o   What does this word mean to you personally?

o   How would it feel to bring this word into daily life?

o   Where is this already present in your life? Where is it missing?

As an example:

My three words:

1. **Authenticity** – I want to experience life with no lies, no deception, and no crafting myself for other people or because of how I think others want me to be.

2. **Creativity** – do something that's not; do things that are different and fill space with things that haven't been thought of or invented. Break habits.

3. **Vitality** – means alive; the opposite of vitality is dead. Do things that create a positive and sustainable life. Shine and portray your light to others!

Gentle Prompt:

Adopt a mantra, a reminder every day, for example … "Today, at least for myself and one other person, I will BE … **AUTHENTIC, CREATIVE, AND VITAL."**

"How can I live these three words today—in small, meaningful ways?"

You may choose to write these words somewhere visible—on a mirror, in your planner, on your phone lock screen—so they become daily reminders of the person, the Human **BE ing** you're **BE coming** ……. **the person you want TO BE** with your behaviour as the **BE** you now **HAVE**

Don't forget, you are not becoming someone new. You are just remembering who you've always been.

Before you go, consider taking the first TWO lists you completed and tear them up, burn them, or dispose of them however you'd like. This THIRD LIST of WORDS are the ones that can now define the Essence of the True You. Reflect on the new list of words that can now define the essence of your true self, and, in adopting these words, you have already begun shaping your new self.

Final task: Living Your 'BE' Words

Now that you have chosen the four words that describe what you want to *BE* in your life, it's time to take the next step in fully embodying them. Previously, I suggested you craft a daily mantra—something like:

"Every day, I will aim to be Authentic, Creative, and Vital for myself and at least one other person."

This next exercise is not about perfection but about practice. Don't worry if you don't remember every day—just *try*. Progress comes through intention and repetition.

Here's what to do next:

1. **Revisit your four 'BE' words** – Read them aloud. Sit with them. Feel their meaning and energy.

2. **Create a new daily mantra** that includes all four words. Let it reflect how you wish to show up for yourself and others.

3. **Practice BEhaving in alignment** with those words each day. Ask yourself: **"How can I act in a way today that reflects who**

I truly want to BE?"

4. **Reflect regularly** – At the end of the day or week, think back: *When did I live into my words?* **Where did I drift? What helped or got in the way?**

You've already done powerful work by choosing your 'BEing' voice. Now, by listening to yourself and consciously aligning your BEhavior (BE-having) with your intention, you'll deepen your transformation.

Keep showing up for yourself. You're BEcoming the person you set out to BE - one choice at a time.

That's a powerful and deeply personal message—one that invites reflection and action. Here's how we could shape that into an inspirational instruction that ties beautifully into your earlier "BE" practice:

Claiming Your Life Legacy Now - Writing Your Own Headstone

Let me offer you this truth:

It's either someone else who gets to write your legacy (for example, your 'headstone'), or you can write it yourself.

Just as you've taken ownership of your *'BE'* words—those guiding principles you strive to embody daily—you now have the chance to define how you'll be remembered, not by leaving it to chance or to someone else's interpretation, but by writing your own headstone.

You might say something like again as an example:

> **Here Lies a Man Who Was True to Himself**
>
> He lived boldly, loved deeply, and left nothing unsaid.
>
> His spirit lives on in the courage to be real, the joy of doing the unexpected, and the quiet moments of gratitude for simply being alive.

This is more than a memorial. It's a daily compass.

Here's your next step:

1. **Write your own headstone.**

   Be bold. Be honest. Capture not just how you hope to be remembered—but how you intend to live right now.

2. **Connect it to your BE words.**

   How does your headstone reflect the person you're becoming? Let this be a powerful mirror that shows your commitment to being that version of yourself.

3. **Revisit it often.**

   Let your headstone remind you that the life you lead today is the legacy you leave tomorrow. Use it to inspire your actions, decisions, and how you show up for others.

4. **Let your spirit be contagious.**

   The words you live by and the way you live them will leave an invisible imprint on others. That's the *Spirit* you pass on—not only when you're gone, but every day you choose to BE fully you.

The Ongoing Journey

BE coming your true self is not a final achievement—it is an unfolding. A spiral. A sacred remembering.

There will be seasons of clarity and seasons of confusion. You will rise, fall, and rise again. But through it all, your essence remains—your steady flame, guiding you home.

Reflect your own wisdom back to you.

Trust your pace.

Honor your path.

And know this: every step you take in the direction of your truth is a step toward freedom.

About The Author

Richard Davies has dedicated over four decades to the mental health industry, beginning his career in the early 1980s after completing psychiatric nurse training and becoming a registered nurse in New South Wales, Australia. His initial experiences at a state mental hospital highlighted the limitations of outdated institutional approaches, an experience that fueled his commitment to seeking more progressive models of care. Throughout his career, Richard has held a variety of clinical roles across the mental health spectrum, including work in acute care teams, emergency departments, and collaborations with the Police, Ambulance, and Clinical Emergency Response (PACER) Team. These diverse experiences have given him a comprehensive perspective on mental health crises and reinforced his belief in the need for innovative, compassionate, and person-centered care.

In 1993, Richard made a significant pivot by founding Asset Risk Management Limited, a publicly listed company specializing in developing systems for managing human, intellectual, and technological resources. He emphasizes that the principles he applied in the corporate sector, strategic thinking, leadership, and effective resource management, are just as vital when nurturing people and shaping organizational culture.

His leadership and service have been recognized by Rotary

International, which awarded him the Paul Harris Fellowship in 2000 for his role in directing the Rotary Youth Leadership Awards in Sydney during the 1990s. Reflecting on his work with young adults, he recalls working with individuals from affluent backgrounds who, despite outward success, carried a deep sense of emptiness and lacked the fulfillment needed to reach their true potential.

Drawing from his extensive experiences, Richard authored "BEcoming the Essence of Your True Self," a book aimed at guiding individuals toward authentic self-awareness and fulfillment. He emphasizes the importance of genuine presence over material possessions or external achievements, stating, "Remember that those in your world need to feel what you are being more than what you have or what you can do for them." His insights encourage a focus on authentic presence and inner growth as the foundation for personal and professional fulfillment.

www.ingramcontent.com/pod-product-compliance
Lightning Source LLC
Chambersburg PA
CBHW050011040726
47599CB00014B/1332